For

Happy Thoughts
for a
SECRET PAL

By Genevieve C. Neff

Illustrated by Wendy Wegner
Designed by Arlene Greco

PETER PAUPER PRESS, INC.
WHITE PLAINS, NEW YORK

Happy Thoughts
for a
SECRET PAL

A good deed,
like sunshine,
will leave you
warm all over.

$\mathcal{L}$aughter does for the soul

what a chocolate chip cookie

does for the stomach.

$\mathcal{W}$hen you give the gift
of friendship, it's never
the wrong size.

A kind word can light up
the day for the giver,
as well as for the recipient.

Share a happy thought with
someone, and see how quickly
you're given one in return.

$\mathcal{A}$ smile can say

more than words.

$\mathcal{F}$ind as many

ways as you can to

show that you care.

Thoughtfulness is

a gift that you can

give without having

to wrap it first.

Share what makes
you happy and see
happiness reflected on
the face of everyone
who looks your way.

Reach out
when you feel down,
and the responses you
receive will lift you up.

$\mathcal{A}$ smile causes

the heart to dance.

$\mathcal{E}$ven a small gesture

of friendship can brighten

someone's day.

$\mathcal{A}$n act of kindness

is an act of caring.

A smile bounces from

one person to another

like a colorful balloon.

$\mathcal{A}$ joyful thought shared

is as satisfying as

a hot fudge sundae,

and has no calories.

An act of compassion

is a gift from one

heart to another.

To share your joy may

not cost anything, but the

recipient knows its value.

$\mathcal{A}$ smile gently hugs

the heart of the one

who receives it.

Happiness emanates
from the most important
parts of you—your heart
and your soul.

If a smile had to be bought,

not even the very rich

could afford one.

The sun would still shine
if no one cared, but our
world would be a much
drearier place.

$\mathcal{A}$ny situation

can be improved with an

encouraging word.

$\mathcal{A}$ mind full of
happy thoughts is a
bounty to be shared.

To express yourself

to a friend is to

reach out and hold

hands with the universe.

$\mathcal{A}$ smile can open doors

that were securely closed.

$\mathscr{B}$lessings are treasures

meant to be shared.

$\mathcal{A}$ flower may wilt,

but the memory

of a helping hand

never fades.

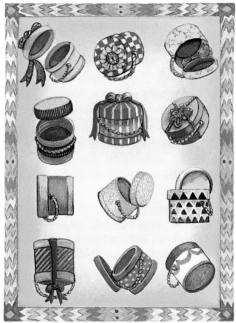

Everyone is beautiful

when sharing laughter.

*G*ray skies clear

when a smile appears.

Thoughtfulness has a sweet
language all its own.

There is nothing that feeds
the heart so well as sincerity.

$\mathcal{A}$ happy thought
shared turns an ordinary
day into one that shines
in your memory.

$\mathcal{A}$ smile kisses your lips

with happiness.

$\mathcal{A}$n act of kindness

radiates outward,

like ripples in a pond,

in ever-growing circles.

If you are kind at every
opportunity, you'll soon find
that kindness abounds.

$\mathcal{E}$very person is special,

and has a special role

to play on this earth.

A smile may
succeed where a
thousand words
might fail.

Those who appear to
be in need will benefit
from your compassion,
but so too may those who
seem not to be in need.

When you embrace

happiness you have

the possibility of

achieving every desire.

The only adornment you
really need is a genuine smile.

$\mathcal{A}$n act of kindness

given freely is a present

more precious than rubies.

*S*mile and see the faces

around you brighten.

Who can resist the urge
to return immediately
the gift of a sincere smile?

Happy thoughts, like stars sprinkled in the sky, are the twinkling moments that illuminate our lives.

$\mathcal{N}$o matter how many
smiles you get, each one
is a new delight.

*E*very day that you are

thankful for life's blessings

is a good day.

$\mathcal{A}$ smile is an embrace

from one soul to another.

$\mathcal{Y}$our thoughtfulness

is the perfect gift no matter

what the occasion.

The best time to

think good thoughts about

someone is—now.

$\mathscr{A}$ happy thought is

music to the soul.

$\mathcal{Y}$ou never have
to look far to find
a reason to share happiness.

Friendship is a gift tied with
an invisible golden bow.

When you smile at
an acquaintance, you
open the possibility
of a new friendship.

It's hard to give
away a smile; it usually
is returned in the
flash of an eye.

A reassuring glance or word refreshes the spirit as though it were washed by a gentle shower.

Happiness makes your feet
step lively, as though a band
were playing to the beat of
your heart.

A single smile
can free the mind of worry
better than any number
of reassuring words.

Showing that you care is the

essence of being human.

$\mathcal{B}$e patient and avoid a

hundred disputes.

$\mathcal{I}$f you engage in a
genuine conversation,
it shows a willingness
to allow another
into your heart.

$\mathcal{Y}$ou'll never regret

sharing a smile

with a friend.

When you bestow
a kindness, you increase
the happiness of
both parties.

Replace a dreaded
thought that enters
your mind with a happy
moment recalled.

$\mathcal{E}$ven a child can

understand a smile.

$\mathscr{A}$ day without kindness
will be gloomy no matter how
much the sun shines.

The act of caring is not

meant to be measured.

$\mathcal{A}$ smile is never an ending

but always a

beautiful beginning.